Some
Things
I've
Learned

CURTIS HUTSON

Some Things I've Learned

Sword of the Lord
Publishers

Printed and bound in the United States of America

Left to right, back row: Dustin Janney, Jana Kay Camperson, Dr. Hutson, Alan Camperson, Gerri Hutson, Tenille Hutson, Tyler Chandler, Diana Janney; Left to right, front row: Derek Janney, Curt Camperson, Denille Janney

Tara Lynn Hutson   Hutson Taylor Chandler

Dedicated to my eleven wonderful grandchildren who have brought inexpressible joy and happiness to my heart. I now think I know what Dr. John R. Rice meant when he said, "If I had known grandchildren were so much fun, I would have had them first."

I pray the simple lessons in this book will help them to live more productive, fruitful, effective Christian lives and help them to be the best persons they can possibly be.

God bless you, Dustin, Alan, Diana, Denille, Curt, Derek, Tyler, Tenille, Jana Kay, Tara Lynn and little Hutson Taylor. PaPa loves you very much.

Since this book is published shortly after the Homegoing of Dr. Curtis Hutson, we felt that it would be of great interest and add significantly to the book to have a candid picture of him at the beginning of every chapter. For those who knew and loved Dr. Hutson, we trust these pictures will be a pleasant reminder of the things they learned from him; and to those who never had the privilege of knowing Dr. Hutson, we hope the pictures will show a man of love and concern who enjoyed being with his family and with other people and who lived life to the fullest.

Contents

Foreword

At the time of the publication of this book, I have been traveling and preaching in churches, conferences, schools and seminars for more than twenty years. In recent years I have driven to many of my meetings. These lessons on living, for the most part, were dictated while I was driving to and from meetings. As a matter of fact, this Foreword is being dictated as I drive to West Virginia for a conference on soul winning and revival.

The things in this book are not intended to be deep theological discussions or eye-opening revelations. I make no claim for originality. Everything I know I've learned; and, simply put, this book contains SOME THINGS I'VE LEARNED.

Whenever I learn things that help me, I try to write them indelibly on the wall of my memory. Life should be governed by principles, not preferences. This book contains some of the simple little principles that were important to me and I pray will be to many others.

Curtis Hutson
[July, 1934–March, 1995]

Introduction

One of the great privileges I have enjoyed in the ministry has been the opportunity to glean wisdom from the minds of wise, godly men. I treasure the drive from the airport, the sandwich after the service, the ride to and from the motel, the meal together. Although my formal training ended with college, I have enjoyed hours of post-graduate work, more helpful than any university course, at the feet of spiritual giants from whom I have learned invaluable lessons.

Of all the great men of God I have been honored to know and learn from, I have enjoyed no one more than Dr. Curtis Hutson. I have questioned him in person, on the phone, and by mail. I have sat open-mouthed in amazement at his wisdom. After an evening in his presence, I have felt compelled to call someone immediately and share the tremendous truths I had just learned. There have been many times when I could not wait to put the practical principles he had just imparted to me into practice. Sleep was an unwelcome intrusion, so consuming and exciting were the ideas he shared with me.

This book gives you a rare and valuable opportunity to delve into the mind of one of the wisest and most greatly used Christians of our generation. Some chapters will make you smile, some may make you grimace as you realize how badly you have done in certain areas, some will elicit a "Wow!"; but all of them will help you.

For many years I maintained that Curtis Hutson had the best blend of biblical content and evangelistic zeal of any preacher I knew. He combined the profound with the practical, information with inspiration, and meat with motivation.

But there is always a man behind every message, and the character of the man is more important than the content of the message.

Dr. Hutson was more than a man who preached great messages. He was a great man whose amazing mind and godly heart combined to produce great messages. This book lets us peek past the sermons and into the spirit and character that gave such impact to his ministry.

For over thirty years Curtis Hutson pointed people to Jesus. As a soul winner, he won thousands to the Saviour. As pastor of the great Forrest Hills Baptist Church and as an evangelist, he saw many thousands more trust Christ. As editor of the SWORD OF THE LORD, he not only made the Gospel plain but challenged us to keep after our main job of winning souls. In all of his life and ministry, he endeavored to fix people's attention on Jesus.

In these pages you will find great philosophy, great methodology and great insights. But you will find something more: you will find a great Saviour and a man who loved Him greatly. I know it was Dr. Hutson's deepest desire that this book, as all his efforts, would make you love and serve the Lord Jesus more than ever. I know he sought, above all, the glory and honor of our wonderful Lord.

Dr. R. B. Ouellette
Pastor, First Baptist Church
Bridgeport, Michigan

The Editor

1

Live one day at a time.

Most people live either in the past or in the future. They're talking about how it used to be or how it's going to be someday and, in so doing, miss life altogether.

Jesus said in Matthew 6:34, "Sufficient unto the day is the evil thereof." In other words, don't borrow from tomorrow.

Someone suggested that worrying is using today's strength on tomorrow's problems.

Years ago I read this little adage, "Yesterday is a canceled check; tomorrow is a promissory note; today is the only cash you have, so spend it wisely."

A friend once asked, "Do you know how to eat an elephant?"

"No," I replied.

And he smiled and said, "One bite at a time."

Years ago I saw a church sign which read, "Yard by yard is mighty hard, but inch by inch is a cinch."

The Bible promises in Deuteronomy 33:25, "...and as thy days, so shall thy strength be."

Dr. Tom Malone once said, "I'm glad He didn't say, 'As thy strength, so shall thy days be.'"

God had a special plan.

2

Stay in your field.

Dr. Bob Jones, Sr., is remembered for his one-sentence sermons and attention-getters, one of which is, "Stay in your field."

In Philippians 3:13 Paul said, "This one thing I do...." One of the secrets of Paul's great life was the fact that he practiced a life of concentration. He did not spread himself too thin by getting involved in too many things. He was first and foremost a preacher and a soul winner.

Andrew Carnegie, addressing a group of young men, said, "Young men, you've heard it said, 'Do not put all your eggs in one basket.' But I say, 'Do put all your eggs in one basket, and mind that basket!'"

Many a person fails in life because he takes on too many things. The secret of success is finding the one thing, the God-appointed thing, and giving it your very best shot.

Have you ever noticed a lion tamer in a cage with a lion? He'll usually have a whip in one hand and a chair in the other. He holds the back of the chair and punches the four legs toward the lion.

There's a reason for this. Somewhere I read that it keeps the lion confused. He doesn't know which leg of the chair to attack. He'll hit at one and then the other and never really concentrate on either. If the lion tamer used a broomstick, the lion would not be confused as to what to attack and would immediately slap the broomstick out of his hand.

When a golfer approaches the ball with two or three different clubs in his hand, it's not likely that he's going to have a good shot. Why? Because he hasn't made up his mind. He's undecided.

"Stay in your field" simply means to find God's will for your life, and don't be sidetracked into doing something else, but rather give your whole life to the God-appointed thing.

A man once boasted that he could whip anybody on his street. No one challenged him. Later he boasted that he could whip anyone in his community, and again no one challenged him. He then said, "I can whip anybody in this county." Still no one challenged him.

One day he boasted to his friends that he could whip anyone in the state. Word got out to surrounding counties, and a few days later a big, rough man from an adjoining county came over and gave the man the whipping of his life.

A few days later a friend saw him. Both eyes were black. His face was bruised and swollen. His friend said, "What in the world happened to you?"

And the battered man said, "I took on too much territory."

Always happy to sign Bibles

3

Go the extra mile.

In Matthew 5:41 Jesus said, "And whosoever shall compel thee to go a mile, go with him twain." I am told that, when the passage was written, the Jews were under the bondage of Rome and that a Roman soldier could compel a Jewish boy to carry his pack for one mile. I've also read that Jewish boys would go out one mile in every direction and mark the spot; then, when a Roman soldier compelled him to carry the pack, he would take it to that spot and drop it, as if to say, "That's all I have to do, and I'm not carrying it a step further."

Jesus said this was not the Christian attitude. He said, 'If you're compelled to go one mile, go twain.'

I refer to this as the "second-mile philosophy," doing more than you have to, doing more than is expected. It is one of the great secrets of success.

Years ago I read this little statement, "The man who succeeds in life is the man who does more than is necessary and keeps on doing it."

E. J. Daniels once said, "Show me a man who's looking for payday and sundown, and I'll show you a man who will not get very far in life."

It's the second-miler who makes himself indispensable to the boss and company. It's the second-miler who has a happy marriage and good relationships.

First Corinthians 15:58 says, "...always abounding in the work of the Lord, forasmuch as ye know that your labour is not in vain in the Lord." The word abound means "more than enough." So here the Bible is teaching the second-mile philosophy—always doing more than enough in the work of the Lord, going the extra mile, doing the unexpected.

People usually do not appreciate you for doing what you're expected to do but rather for doing the unexpected. A wife very seldom, if ever, thanks her husband for paying the house note, furnishing money for groceries, utilities, clothes and all the other big items. He's expected to do this. This is going the first mile. But if that same husband brings home a dozen roses for some special occasion, she tells all her friends about it. Why? Because he's done the unexpected; he's gone the second mile.

A chaplain in the army noticed that some men in his company missed their wives more than others. So he set out to find out why. In interviewing the men who seemed to miss their wives the most, he asked, "What is it you miss about your wife?"

To his surprise, it wasn't the big things but the little, unexpected things. One man said, "My wife shampooed my hair every Saturday night. It was something I looked forward to. And when Saturday night comes, I think about it."

Another man said his wife manicured his nails. Another mentioned the fact that his wife would rub his shoulders a few minutes every night after he would come home from a hard day's work. In each case it was something small, something unexpected, where the wife had gone the second mile. The second-mile wives were missed the most.

If you want to make your boss and company proud of you, don't just do what's expected: go the extra mile and do a little more than they expect. If you want to make your parents happy, go the extra mile and do more than they expect.

When I was pastor of a small church in Atlanta, Georgia, I was aware that I did not have the educational background of other preachers in the area. So I reasoned,

They may be more educated than I am. They may be better speakers. And for the most part, they may have better personalities. But not a preacher in town has more time in a day than I have. And I can work as hard as any of them.

I soon learned that the margin of success was going the extra mile. I spent more time visiting, calling on people and winning souls. I've often passed some of those preachers' homes and seen them relaxing in their backyards while I was still out making calls. As a result of going the extra mile, we saw that tiny church grow from thirty or forty members to over 8,000 members and become the largest church in the state of Georgia; and, in 1972, the fastest growing church in the nation, increasing our attendance 846 per Sunday over the 1971 average.

In the last five years we were there, the church was the largest and fastest growing in the state. One of the secrets: going the extra mile.

4

"It's in the genes!"
(Jana Kay Camperson)

Don't quit.

The difference between winners and losers is not talent but determination. One of Andrew Jackson's boyhood friends said, "I could throw Andrew nine times out of ten, but he wouldn't stay 'throwed.'" In other words, he wouldn't quit. He kept getting up.

A football coach put two players on the field and asked one to tackle the other, then instructed the other to do his best to keep from being tackled. The one instructed to do the tackling knocked his opponent down in a moment. The opponent got up again and was immediately knocked down. As fast as he could get up, the bigger, stronger boy knocked him down.

He was knocked down so many times that he could hardly get up, but he kept getting up. Finally the coach stopped the two and then addressed the football team and said, "Now, that's the way I want you to be."

One young man excitedly said, "You mean like Bill?" who could tackle Jim immediately and kept tackling him time and time again.

"No," said the coach, "I want you to be like Jim. Keep getting up no matter how many times you're tackled."

There's a little statement I remember reading in one of my schoolbooks forty years ago. It simply said, "If at first you don't succeed, try and try again."

Abraham Lincoln said, "I do the very best I know how—the very best I can—and I mean to keep doing so." His life is the best example of his own words. Consider the chronology of his career:

> 1831—Failed in business
> 1832—Defeated for legislature
> 1833—Again failed in business
> 1834—Elected to legislature

1835—Sweetheart died
1836—Had nervous breakdown
1838—Defeated for speaker
1840—Defeated for elector
1843—Defeated for Congress
1846—Elected to Congress
1848—Defeated for Congress
1855—Defeated for Senate
1856—Defeated for Vice-President
1858—Defeated for Senate
1860—ELECTED PRESIDENT

Dr. Lee Roberson said that Dr. Faulkner visited one family more than sixty times, trying to get them to come to church. After sixty-something visits, the couple finally came. They were both saved. As a result, many others were won to the Saviour.

I recall witnessing to one man fifteen or twenty times. As a matter of fact, I had almost given up on him. I decided to go by and make one more visit. When he answered the door, I said, "Bill, I felt I should come by and visit you one more time. Don't you think it's about time you trusted Christ as your Saviour?"

To which he replied, "I don't see why I should wait any longer." Then and there he trusted Christ. The next Sunday he joined the church, and I baptized him. He made a faithful member, donated money to the church and helped us with many important projects.

When Mohammed Ali fought Joe Frazier in Manilla, a fight which became known as "the thrilla' in Manilla," he barely pulled out a victory. After the fight Ali said that Frazier had hit him so hard and so many times that he felt he was completely gone. He had hardly any strength left.

Near the end of the fight he almost gave up. With only a few rounds left, Ali said, "I went to the well one more time." In other words, he refused to quit and in the last few rounds edged out a victory.

Dr. Bob Jones, Sr., wisely said, "The test of a man's character is what it takes to stop him." Refuse to give up. Keep trying. Don't quit.

It's not the size of the dog in the fight but the size of the fight in the dog that matters.

Youthful glimpses

Make stepping-stones out of stumbling blocks.

5

A young boy was leading his baby sister up a rugged hill. "Come on," he said. "Follow me. I'll lead you in the path." After awhile it seemed like the path completely disappeared and was filled with nothing but stones.

Stumbling and falling, the little girl began to cry and said, "This is no path at all. It is nothing but stones."

To which her confident brother replied, "The stones are for climbing."

When some people run into stones along life's pathway, they complain. They seem to think they're the only ones who've ever had problems.

Others not only complain, they kick against the stones to their own hurt. Some get discouraged and refuse to carry on. They sit down and stop altogether.

And sad to say, some not only complain, kick against the stones and refuse to carry on, but go back, giving up all progress heretofore made.

But some precious souls discover that the stones are for climbing and one by one put the stones under their feet and rise higher and higher.

An old adage says, "We rise by the things we put under our feet."

The story is told of a man's horse which fell into a deep pit. The man tried everything he knew to get the horse out, but with no success. Finally he decided to cover the horse with dirt. One shovelful at a time he threw dirt down into the deep pit.

But instead of being buried, the horse shook the dirt off, and it fell beneath his feet. Little by little the horse began to rise; and when the hole was filled, the horse was standing on level ground. He had risen by the things he had put under his feet.

A preacher told the story of making stepping-stones out of stumbling blocks. He was pastor of a small church with hardly any facilities for Sunday school. The church grew so fast that they had no place to put the people. Scores of boys and girls didn't have chairs to sit on.

One Sunday, while the children were complaining, the preacher excitedly said, "I know what we will do! Let's have Japanese Sunday school." And he explained that in Japan people sat on the floor. Then he proceeded to demonstrate how they did it.

One by one the children all found a place on the floor. In a few minutes they were totally engrossed in the lesson.

The following week they invited their friends to attend their Japanese Sunday school. And until the church could afford chairs, they simply sat on the floor and listened to the lesson. And the teacher sat down with them.

Remember, the stones are for climbing.

The chief attraction at PaPa's beautiful
farm is still PaPa!
(Dustin Janney)

6

Don't let failure discourage you.

I t is impossible to succeed without failing. This may seem like a contradiction, but those who have experienced the greatest success have known the greatest failures. The man who never fails is the one who never attempts anything. And the more one attempts, the more he fails. But the more he fails, the more he'll learn. And the more he puts into practice what he's learned, the more he will succeed.

So to quote Dr. Bob Jones, Sr., again, "Make chariot wheels out of your failures, and ride them to success." I've never learned anything from my successes; all I've learned is from my failures. Failure is opportunity for improvement. When you discover something will not work, try something else. If that doesn't work, then try something else. Sooner or later you'll find the solution.

I have read that Thomas Edison, when trying to invent the light bulb, tried 700 things that failed. Finally a friend said to him, "Mr. Edison, you have failed 700 times. Why don't you quit?"

To which Edison replied, "I have not failed 700 times; I've discovered 700 things that won't work in a light bulb." He is responsible for more than 1,100 inventions which we enjoy today, including the light bulb.

And by the way, a friend of mine told me that he visited Edison's home, and there was a light bulb still burning that was made by Thomas Edison himself.

Do you remember trying to learn to ride the bicycle? Did you ride it perfectly the first time? Of course you didn't. Like everyone else, you fell. And if your experience was like mine, it didn't feel good. But you wanted to learn to ride, so you tried again. And you probably fell again and again until finally you were able to balance yourself and ride for a long distance without falling.

You eventually got to where you could ride without holding the handlebars. Every failure was a learning experience, and you never would have succeeded if you hadn't failed. So don't let failure discourage you. It is the stuff of which success is made.

7

"Dear Jesus, please give me the message You have for these people."

Work at making friends.

G. Campbell Morgan once said, "A man has many acquaintances in life, but few friends." On the wall in our home is a piece of needlework which reads, "Friends are like jewels, precious and rare; but acquaintances are like leaves, scattered everywhere."

You don't have to explain to friends. You don't have to impress friends. You don't have to put on a facade for friends. Friends want you to be yourself around them. Friends understand. You can confide in friends. Friends are faithful. Friends understand when you feel bad and don't feel like talking. Your enemies won't believe your explanations, and your friends don't need them.

The Bible says in Proverbs 17:17, "A friend loveth at all times...." And Proverbs 18:24 declares, "A man that hath friends must shew himself friendly...." Proverbs 27:10 reminds us, "Thine own friend, and thy father's friend, forsake not...."

The Scripture tells us in Proverbs 27:17, "Iron sharpeneth iron; so a man sharpeneth the countenance of his friend."

How do we make friends? Well, I've already shared the Scripture that says, "A man that hath friends must shew himself friendly." You must be a friend to make a friend. You don't attract what you *want;* you attract what you *are.*

Another suggestion is found in Proverbs 19:6: "...and every man is a friend to him that giveth gifts." I'm thinking now of one of my own dear friends, and it just occurred to me that I only see him two or three times a year; and nearly every time I do, he has some

43

gift for me. Oh, it's not some expensive thing but some little something he saw and thought I might enjoy.

He's not trying to buy my friendship. He has too much character for that. But rather, he's trying to demonstrate his friendship to me. He reminds me often, "I am your friend." And I believe him.

It's not the things he gives but the thoughtfulness he demonstrates. I notice when I am around him that he has many other friends, and I've often heard men refer to him as "my friend." He has a lot of friends because he does those things the Bible says one must do to have friends.

Two sweethearts
(Denille Janney)

8

Try not to make enemies.

Several years ago I read a book entitled *The World's Greatest Salesman*. The author sold more automobiles than anyone else in the world. In the book he said something to the effect that one should be careful not to make enemies. He went on to explain that every person has approximately 200 people that he or she can influence. He got that number by getting an average of the number of people who attend one's wedding and funeral and concluded that, if someone thought enough of you to attend your wedding or funeral, he was close enough to be influenced by you.

The author explained that, when you make an enemy, you usually make enemies out of 200 other individuals over whom he has influence. If someone doesn't like you, then every time your name comes up around his friends, he is likely to say something negative about you. And since his friends do not know you, the only impression they have of you is what they get from their friend. So until they learn better, which they very seldom ever do, they keep the negative impression received from their friend.

A person in a small town who makes several enemies may soon discover that very few people in town like him.

Of course, the opposite is also true. If you leave a positive impression with an individual, then he has 200 friends who are likely to get a positive impression of you, because every time your name comes up among his friends, he will say, "Oh, yes, I know him. He's a good man."

I'm not suggesting that you can go through life

without making enemies. Moving parts always create friction. And the man who has no enemies is one who says nothing, does nothing and is nothing.

But what I am suggesting is that we try our best not to make enemies. Romans 12:18 says, "If it be possible, as much as lieth in you, live peaceably with all men." The Scripture says, "If it be possible." In other words, sometimes it's not possible. But be sure you've done everything you possibly can to live at peace with all men—in the words of the Scripture, "...as much as lieth in you...." If you're not at peace with an individual, make sure it's not because you haven't exhausted every effort and avenue to do so.

The next time you're tempted to make some sharp remark to an individual, thinking he doesn't matter anyway, remember that he probably has 200 people whom he can influence. When you leave him, make sure that he'll go away to tell his friends good things about you and not bad things.

Heading home after a meeting

9

Enjoy the good things the Lord has given you.

For the most part, there's nothing wrong with *things* but rather the *place* things occupy in our lives. In Matthew 6:33 Jesus said, "But seek ye first the kingdom of God, and his righteousness; and all these *things* shall be added unto you." Here the Lord does not speak prohibitively of things but rather the *place* things occupy in our lives.

In the preceding verses, the *things* He refers to are food and clothing, the basic necessities of life. There's certainly nothing wrong with having food and clothing. One should enjoy both. But even the basic necessities of life can become sinful if we give them the wrong place.

The text clearly teaches that we're not to seek food and clothing but rather "Seek ye first the kingdom of God, and his righteousness"—that is, seek the control of God over your life and the character of God in your life; or to put it another way, seek the rule of God over your life and the righteousness of God in your life. And Jesus promises that these other things—food and clothing—will be added unto you.

A man who lives only for fine clothes and good food has his priorities wrong. A diamond ring on a lady's finger is a beautiful thing to behold. But put that same diamond ring in her high-heeled shoe and let her walk a few steps, and the thing that brought pleasure on the finger brings pain in the shoe. It's the same diamond ring. The only difference is the place it is occupying.

As long as a person keeps his or her priorities right, there's nothing wrong with enjoying *things*. There's nothing wrong with enjoying a good baseball game, but you wouldn't want to go to a baseball game when you should be in church on Sunday morning or Sunday night. There's nothing wrong with using one's money to buy something that he or she would enjoy as long as it's not the tithe, which belongs to the Lord.

Some Christians seem to think that it is sinful to enjoy anything. Somewhere they evidently got the impression that you have to be miserable and unhappy to be a good Christian. The Devil has sold them a false bill of goods. The happiest people in the world ought to be Christians. Dr. John R. Rice once said, "A long face is a poor sign-board for Jesus."

Look at creation. Have you ever seen anything more beautiful than a sunset or a sunrise on a clear morning? Have you ever seen anything more beautiful than wild flowers in the early spring? What about a bird in flight or a swan upon a lake? These are all things that God made, and He made them beautiful for us to enjoy.

How sad, then, that we should go through life and not enjoy things! You're only going to be here for a few years as you are now. Of course, we're coming back someday to reign with Christ, but it will be different then. So while we're here, let's enjoy the things the Lord has given us.

Use the good china. Don't let it sit in a cabinet and then forty or fifty years from now pass it on to your children, who will pass it on to your grandchildren, and no one will ever enjoy it. Use the good silver. Why have it if you can't enjoy it? You're better off to sell it and use the money for something else.

Buy yourself a good mattress and box springs. You spend nearly one-third of your life in bed. That's about twenty-four years. Why should you spend it on a broken-down mattress and springs and get up with a backache every morning? If the Lord has provided so that you can have a nice automobile, enjoy it. If you can afford it, buy a nice easy chair in which to sit, relax and enjoy reading or watching your favorite programs on TV.

I would suggest that periodically you go through the house, collect all the things you're never going to use, have a big yard sale or an auction, then take the money and put it into something you can enjoy.

First Timothy 6:17 says, "Charge them that are rich in this world, that they be not highminded, nor trust in uncertain riches, but in the living God, **who giveth us richly all things to enjoy.**" God said that we are to charge them that are rich that they trust not in uncertain riches. In other words, they're not to put their confidence in things, because things are uncertain. They are here today and gone tomorrow.

But the same verse says God gives us "all things to enjoy." The purpose of having things is not to trust in them but to enjoy them.

To paraphrase the verse: 'Trust in God and enjoy things.'

Money is neither moral nor immoral; it's amoral. It is our attitude toward money which is moral or immoral. The Bible says in I Timothy 6:10, "The love of money is the root of all evil [all kinds of evil]." I know men who have money, but they don't love money. I also know men who do not have money, but they love money. They collect money the way a person collects postage stamps. They would go hungry and do without things they need before they would spend a dime.

A man who has enough money to live in a comfortable home but lives in a shack, and his family does without, is not conservative; he's greedy. I'm not suggesting that one be wasteful, but I am suggesting that a person learn to enjoy the things God has given him.

Remember, that's why they were given.

Gerri and Curtis Hutson

10

Be quick to admit when you're wrong.

There are no perfect people. Everybody makes mistakes. As soon as you know you're wrong, admit it—the quicker, the better.

Richard Nixon had to resign the presidency, not because he was wrong, but because he wouldn't admit it. Burglarizing the Watergate Hotel was no major thing. No one was hurt, no one was killed, and nobody lost anything. Yet it cost Richard Nixon the presidency. If he had issued a statement immediately, saying, "Yes, some of my men broke into the Watergate Hotel. It was wrong, and I want to get it right," he would have served out his term and not had to resign.

I have known preachers, whose names I will not use, to lose their ministries simply because they would not admit they were wrong. Rather than admitting they were wrong, they tried to excuse their behavior, justify their actions or discredit the person who called attention to their mistake.

If you're wrong with your wife, admit it and put it behind you. If you're wrong with your children, admit it and put it behind you. If you're wrong with your parents, admit it and put it behind you. The sooner, the better.

In reading the Bible, I have discovered things people do with their sins: first, they try to blame someone else. This is the case with the first man who ever sinned. When God asked Adam why he had taken of the forbidden fruit, he said, "The woman whom thou gavest to be with me, she gave me of the tree, and I did eat." In other words, "It's not my fault; it was Eve's fault and really Your fault, because You're the one who gave me the woman."

The second thing people do with their sins is hide them. This is the case of Achan, in the Old Testament, who was told not to take the accursed thing; but he took the gold and silver and other things and hid them in his tent.

But wrong cannot be hidden long. Sooner or later it will come to the surface unless it's dealt with in a scriptural manner.

A third thing people do about their sins is try to justify them. This is the case of Saul in the Old Testament. He disobeyed God and kept things that God told him to destroy. When he was asked why he disobeyed the Lord, he explained, 'I kept these prize sheep and prize cattle to have something to sacrifice unto the Lord.'

And the prophet said, "To obey is better than sacrifice, and to hearken than the fat of rams" (I Sam. 15:22).

The fourth thing I find in the Bible that men do with their sins is the right thing—that is, confess them. First John 1:9 says, "If we confess our sins, he is faithful and just to forgive us our sins, and to cleanse us from all unrighteousness." So as soon as you know you're wrong, admit it—not only to those you've wronged, but confess it to Christ as a sin, that you may obtain His forgiveness and cleansing as He has clearly promised in I John 1:9.

"You're a good crowd."

Discipline yourself to read.

Paul said to Timothy in I Timothy 4:13, "Give attendance to reading...." A friend of mine, Charles Tremendous Jones, said, "You're the same person right now you'll be this same time next year except for the people you meet and the books you read." Readers are leaders.

The first among all books is the Bible; therefore, it should be at the top of the list of everybody's priority reading material. D. L. Moody said, "When we pray, we talk to God; when we read the Bible, God talks to us; and we need to do most of the listening." The Bible should be read through every year.

G. Campbell Morgan, the twentieth century's greatest expositor, once said from the pulpit, "The Bible can be read through in sixty hours." After the service, one of his members, a banker, disagreed with him, saying that he did not believe the statement. Morgan simply replied, "Then the burden of proof lies with you."

A few weeks later he came back and said, "Mr. Morgan, you were wrong about that statement that the Bible could be read through in sixty hours."

"Yes?" Morgan asked as he waited for further comment.

The man said, "It can be read through in forty hours," to which G. Campbell Morgan replied, "I was not talking about bankers' rates: I was talking about pulpit rate."

But at pulpit rate, the Bible could be read through in sixty hours; yet few people ever read it through. If you set out to read three chapters a day and four chapters every third day, you can read through the Bible in one year. And few things can be more rewarding.

In addition to the Bible, one should read good books. But don't waste time reading things that are not constructive and helpful. Biographies of great men are good reading. I encourage young people everywhere to read biographies.

They'll do several things for you: first, you'll discover that God uses ordinary men to accomplish extraordinary things. Second, you'll learn little but important things about the men that made them great. Third, seeing what other men have accomplished will build your faith and cause you to believe that God could use you in like manner.

Lives of great men all remind us
We, too, can make our lives sublime;
And, in passing, leave behind us
Footprints on the sands of time.

The Bible says in Proverbs 13:20, "He that walketh with wise men shall be wise: but a companion of fools shall be destroyed." In a sense, when you read biographies of great men, you're walking with the wise.

Read sermons. Some of the best literature in the world is sermons, especially the older sermons by men like T. DeWitt Talmage, Charles Haddon Spurgeon and others. Be sure you read after fundamental Christians and not after modernists who deny the Bible is the Word of God.

As editor of the SWORD OF THE LORD and president of the Foundation, I highly recommend all Sword books—especially Dr. John R. Rice's sermons and commentaries, Tom Malone's sermons, as well as sermon books by others.

When a person is an adult, he should start reading a reliable newspaper every day, keeping up with current events and what's going on in the world. When you read, try to remember statistics and facts so that, when you need them, you can quote them accurately. If you can't read as much as you would like to, then at least keep abreast of the most important things happening in the world.

When you read, make notes in the margins of your books of thoughts that come to mind. Reading comes easy for some: they enjoy it. But to others it is labor. But

62

whatever the case may be in your situation, make yourself read anyway. In a sense, you are what you feed on mentally; so feed on good books.

And the best Book of all is the Bible!

This means, "Say Amen."

Cultivate gratitude.

Dr. Bob Jones, Sr., said, "Gratitude is the loveliest flower that grows in the garden of man's soul; and when gratitude dies on the altar of a man's heart, he is well nigh gone." It doesn't cost you anything to be grateful, and it says a lot about your character.

Say "thank you" a lot and mean it: "thank you" to the waitress when she brings tea or coffee or additional water to the table; "thank you" to your mate when he or she does something for you; "thank you" to your mom or dad or to a friend who does something for you. Never take things for granted. Accept them with gratitude.

Jesus tells of ten lepers who were cleansed, and only one turned back to say "thank you." Evidently gratitude was important to Christ, and a simple "thank you" was expected.

Of all the great men I've known personally or read about, I've never known one who was an ingrate.

Ephesians 5:20 says, "Giving thanks always for all things unto God and the Father in the name of our Lord Jesus Christ." And in I Thessalonians 5:18 we read, "In every thing give thanks: for this is the will of God in Christ Jesus concerning you."

We're not only to thank God *for* all things but *in* all things—in every situation, no matter what comes to our lives.

The only way we can do it is to remember another "all things," found in Romans 8:28: "And we know that *all things* work together for good to them that love God, to them who are the called according to his purpose."

When we understand that God has only our good in

mind, we will not find it difficult to thank Him for all things.

A small boy was given a piece of cake, and he immediately said, "Thank you."

"Oh," said the lady, "I like to hear little boys say thank you."

He replied: "Put some ice cream on it, and I'll say it again!"

-13-

"This is great, PaPa! Let's make as much noise as we can!"
(Tyler Chandler)

"Never fight a battle where nothing is accomplished by the victory."

This is a quote from General George Patton's *Lessons for Leaders.* It is very good advice. Most of the fusses and fights that people have in life are not worth having, because nothing is accomplished by the victory.

The husband and wife argue for an hour over who set the glass on the coffee table; and once the argument is settled, nothing is accomplished. As a matter of fact, usually something's lost. The one who wins the argument usually loses the fellowship of the other for several hours, if not for a day or two. Some things are not worth fighting for. We should not waste time or energy even discussing them.

I once said to a group of preachers, "There are some things that I'd die for, other things that I'd fight for that I wouldn't die for, and still other things that I'd fuss about that I wouldn't fight over." It's wise to learn to put everything in one of these categories.

When the Apostle Paul was facing execution, he said in II Timothy 4:7, "I have fought a good fight." He didn't mean that he fought well. That may have been the case, but it wasn't for Paul to say. That was for God to decide.

When he said, "I have fought a good fight," he was saying, 'The cause for which I fought was a good one.'

If you're going to fight, make sure, absolutely sure, that you're fighting for a good cause, or else it isn't a good fight. And never fight a battle where nothing is accomplished through the victory.

Drawing the net

14

Never over-advertise or overstate a matter.

You're better off to understate the matter and have people discover more than they expected, than to overstate it and have them disappointed. Remember what the Queen of Sheba said when she came to see King Solomon: "...behold, the half was not told me..." (I Kings 10:7). She was impressed to find more than she expected.

I've always felt it was to my advantage to lower expectations before I preached than to raise expectations and not live up to them. I have often made such statements as, "I know why Dr. John R. Rice is here: he's the smartest man I've ever known," or, "I know why Dr. Jack Hyles is here speaking. He's the pastor of the largest church in America. But I don't know what I'm doing here. I'm not very smart, and I don't have the largest church in the nation. However, I'll do the best I can."

If people don't expect much, then you don't have to do much to impress them. And if you do more than they expect, then you're a great success. If you're playing golf with a friend, it's best not to make him think that you're a good golfer and then shoot a poor score, but rather have him think that you are not so good and then shoot a good score.

When you overstate the matter, it puts additional pressure on you to try to live up to the person's expectations.

When I was pastor of Georgia's largest church, I tried to advertise so that, when people came, they always found more than they expected. This way they went away talking positively about the ministry rather than making such negative remarks as, "Well, I thought that was a great church. I thought they had great crowds. It certainly wasn't what I thought it was." Produce more than you promise.

Overadvertising produces negative results.

Dear Dr. Rice backed his
chosen successor.

15

Personal
appearance
is important.

People judge you by three things: how you look, how you talk and how you act. And the majority of those judgments or opinions are based solely on your appearance. Of all the people who see you, only a few have the opportunity to hear you talk, and still fewer get to observe the way you act. Therefore, most opinions formed are based solely on your appearance.

A man charged with a crime is usually instructed by a wise lawyer to make the best possible appearance in the courtroom. He doesn't want to come before the jury looking like a criminal but rather like a quiet, nice, decent citizen. Therefore, he usually comes to court wearing a conservative suit and a matching tie and speaks in polite tones.

Why? Because appearance is important. He wants to appear to the jury that he is not a criminal but a good citizen, perhaps even the neighbor next door.

Policemen should look like policemen; marines should look like marines; sailors should look like sailors; and a preacher should look like a preacher.

Give the right appearance. Wear polished shoes. Wear a nice tie. Make sure your clothes are clean and well pressed. Your clothing does not have to be expensive, but it should be neat. Keep your hair neatly groomed. A good haircut, a nice tie, shined shoes and a clean shirt will do a lot to offset a not-so-good suit.

When you're meeting someone for the first time, remember, there's no second chance to make a first impression. The Scripture says in I Samuel 16:7, "Man looketh on the outward appearance...."

Some good people have two strikes against them before they ever say a word because of a poor personal appearance. Before they say or do anything, an incorrect judgment has already been formed, based solely on appearance. They say you can't tell a book by its cover, and that's true. But many good books are never sold because of a poor cover. And many not-so-good books have sold because of a good cover.

"Tenille, tell the people how much
you love PaPa."
(Tenille Hutson)

16

Be forgiving, both of yourself and of others.

When the Lord gave us the pattern prayer, He taught us to pray, "Forgive us our debts, as we forgive our debtors" (Matt. 6:12). Then in verses 14 and 15 He said, "For if ye forgive men their trespasses, your heavenly Father will also forgive you: But if ye forgive not men their trespasses, neither will your Father forgive your trespasses."

It is impossible to be like Christ and not be forgiving. Keep in mind that we do not deserve His forgiveness, but He forgives us anyway. When someone asks forgiveness, immediately assure him that he is forgiven and mean it. This means that you're never to bring it up again—never. For no reason under any circumstances should you ever mention it to the individual again. It is forgiven. I'm not saying you must forget it. That is not always possible. But you should never bring it up again.

To have an unforgiving spirit and harbor bitterness only hurts one's self. Hatred is a poison that destroys the vessel in which it's kept.

Then, too, learn to forgive yourself. Everybody makes mistakes. The problem is not failing, but failing to take advantage of the provision God has made for our failures. First John 1:9 promises, "If we confess our sins, he is faithful and just to forgive us our sins, and to cleanse us from all unrighteousness." Here is the Christian's way to forgiveness and cleansing.

When we confess our sin to Christ, we may know that we're forgiven and cleansed, because that is exactly what He promises in I John 1:9. Once God has forgiven you, then forgive yourself. Assure yourself that God not only forgave you but cleansed you, and the wrong no longer exists; it is gone. So why keep punishing yourself for something that God has forgiven and forgotten?

Isaiah 43:25 says, "I, even I, am he that blotteth out thy transgressions for mine own sake, and will not remember thy sins." Don't worry about things that God Himself has blotted out and forgotten about.

Some people go through life miserable because they will not forgive themselves. So learn to be forgiving, not only of others but also of yourself.

It's always great to get
home for awhile.

17

Give to others what you want for yourself.

've often said that a person can have whatever he wants and as much of it as he wants. I base that on Luke 6:38 where the Scripture says, "Give, and it shall be given unto you; good measure, pressed down, and shaken together, and running over, shall men give into your bosom. For with the same measure that ye mete withal it shall be measured to you again."

Now notice the verse does not say what to give. It just says, "Give, and it shall be given unto you." In other words, if you want love, give love, and love shall be given you. If you want smiles, give smiles, and smiles will be given you. If you want forgiveness, give forgiveness, and forgiveness will be given to you.

Whatever you give is given to you again, but it's important to notice that you get more than you give. When it comes back, it comes back "good measure, pressed down, and shaken together, and running over."

John Bunyan once said,

> **There was a man in our town—**
> **Some folks did think him mad.**
> **The more he gave away,**
> **The more he had.**

If you want folks to speak to you, speak to them. Be the first to say hello. If no one is showing love to you, it's because you're not showing love to others.

Give what you want, and it shall be given to you again, "good measure, pressed down, and shaken together, and running over."

Giving away the youngest
(Kay Chandler)

—18—

Always respect authority.

The Scripture says in Romans 13:1, "Let every soul be subject unto the higher powers. For there is no power but of God: the powers that be are ordained of God."

And the next verse warns, "Whosoever therefore resisteth the power, resisteth the ordinance of God...." God has ordained certain powers and authorities, and we must identify such authorities and submit ourselves.

One authority is our parents. We are plainly told in Ephesians 6:1, "Children, obey your parents in the Lord: for this is right." The expression, "in the Lord," means "as God's appointed representatives over you." In other words, to disobey parents is to disobey God Himself.

The same goes for all authority, whether it be the policeman, the judge, the governor or someone else. We must distinguish between personality and position. We do not have to respect a person who may be immoral and wicked; but if that person holds a position of authority, then we must respect the position.

Children must be taught obedience and submission at home. Dr. John R. Rice once said, "The best way to get rid of criminals is to stop raising them." When a parent allows a child to get by with disrespect and disobedience, the child grows up to have disrespect and to disobey schoolteachers, policemen and others.

The problem with rebellious people and criminals is that they were not taught early to respect authority.

Cultivate a habit of saying, "Yes, sir," "No, sir," "Yes, ma'am" and "No, ma'am," to your parents and grandparents and all others in a position of authority over you.

91

A chain of subscriptions makes a
great birthday gift!

Make time
for prayer.

Prayer is the one thing that Christians are commanded to do without ceasing. They're not told to sing without ceasing or to go to church without ceasing or to read the Bible without ceasing; but they are told in I Thessalonians 5:17, "Pray without ceasing."

The Scripture also says in Luke 18:1, "Men ought always to pray, and not to faint."

Dr. John R. Rice once said, "All your failures are prayer failures." And then he quoted James 4:2, "Ye have not, because ye ask not."

A. J. Gordon said, "There is more you can do *after* you pray, but there is nothing more you can do *until* you pray."

Prayer is God's appointed way of getting things. He said in Matthew 7:7, "Ask, and it shall be given you; seek, and ye shall find; knock, and it shall be opened unto you."

Prayer is God's appointed way to fullness of joy. He said in John 16:24, "Hitherto have ye asked nothing in my name: ask, and ye shall receive, that your joy may be full."

Prayer is God's appointed way to obtain forgiveness and cleansing. First John 1:9 says, "If we confess our sins, he is faithful and just to forgive us our sins, and to cleanse us from all unrighteousness."

Prayer is God's appointed way to obtain victory over anxiety (Phil. 4:6, 7). Prayer is also God's appointed way of our expressing praise and gratitude.

When we pray, God may not do everything we ask

Him to do; but if we don't pray, we don't even give Him a chance. So pray about things that seem utterly impossible to you. It may surprise you what God will do. Remember, the possibilities of prayer exceed your ability to ask or think. Ephesians 3:20 says, "Now unto him that is able to do exceeding abundantly above all that we ask or think...."

"This is heavier than it looks."

20

Surround yourself with beautiful things.

A person's attitude has a lot to do with his altitude. The Scripture says in Proverbs 23:7, "For as he thinketh in his heart, so is he."

One's surroundings can have a lot to do with one's attitude. When I say surround yourself with beautiful things, I don't mean expensive things. Find a picture that you enjoy looking at, and put it in a conspicuous spot. Plant flowers in the springtime so that the landscape looks beautiful. Put live flowers on the table occasionally. Make the place where you eat, a bright, happy-looking place. Use brightly colored dishes or decorations that look good to you. Never mind what others think. Decorate your home for yourself, not others.

You spend a lot of time in your home. Make it a place that you can enjoy to the utmost.

Get a good radio or stereo and listen to beautiful music.

"PaPa, I can't breathe!"
(Derek Janney)

21

Don't give up too easily.

Many people have failed in life because they lacked persistence. As an experiment, a bass and a minnow were placed in a large glass tank. Separating the two was an invisible glass. The hungry bass swam toward the minnow but hit his nose on the glass. He tried again and again and again, but every time he would swim into the glass wall.

After many attempts the bass stopped trying. The glass was then removed, and the minnow was safe, because the bass never again tried to get the minnow. He had given up.

A man was late for his flight and was told by someone in the waiting area that they had already closed the door on the plane and he would have to wait for the next flight. But he ignored the person and continued running up that little walkway toward the plane. On the way he was met by two or three people coming back the other way who told him that he was too late for the flight, that the doors had already been closed.

But he wouldn't take no for an answer. When he reached the end of the loading ramp, the plane was still there. And even though the door was closed, he began to wave his arms and briefcase, trying to get the pilot's attention. Finally the pilot looked in his direction, and he motioned for the pilot to open the door.

At first the pilot shook his head no; but when the man continued, the pilot opened the door and let him in. The man made his flight because he wouldn't take no for an answer.

Don't be too quick to give up. Try again and again and again. Victory may be just around the corner.

22

"Mrs. Rice, you sing; I'll play."

Be a gracious loser.

It is impossible for everybody to win at everything. Sometimes we lose. However, we should not lose because we didn't try.

When I was responsible for a school, I said to our ball players, "I don't mind your losing as long as you played your best. But I hate to lose when I know we could have won."

When you're outmatched, be a gracious loser and compliment your opponent on his victory and good play. Use your defeat as an incentive to practice harder and be better prepared the next time.

Family vacations are always special.
(Derek and Diana Janney and friend)

23

Don't learn the "tricks of the trade"; learn the trade.

A man can be a success in any honest endeavor if he masters his trade. Pray about what you should do with your life; and once you feel that God has led you to some definite endeavor, then give your life to it.

Read all the books you can about your trade or calling. Then spend as much time as you can with those who have been successful in the same area, and get as much advice from them as they'll give. Don't waste your time getting advice from those who fail. You will only learn how to fail, too. Learn from those who are doing it.

Don't look for shortcuts by learning the so-called "tricks of the trade." There is no shortcut to success. That old adage, "Build a better mousetrap, and the world will beat a path to your door," is absolutely true. It applies to the person who prepares a better meal, makes a better suit of clothes, builds a better house, preaches a better sermon, or anything else.

Offer the best in quality and service in whatever you do, and you'll be a success.

I had the occasion to meet one of the wealthiest men in America, and he told me that he never set out to make money. That was never his aim. "I set out to have a better product," he said, "and the money followed."

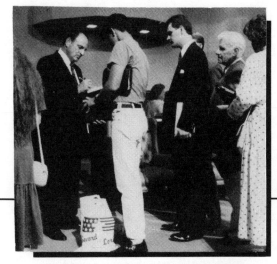

"I'm glad to see that bag of Sword books."

24

Take good care of your health.

I t's easier to retain than it is to regain health. When God created man, He created him to live forever; and had there been no sin, the human body would have been capable of living forever.

The average body consists of 100 trillion cells, and cell life is about 120 days. Each cell has an RNA and DNA which is, in essence, a blueprint so that each cell can reproduce itself as it dies. But, of course, the body cannot reproduce healthy cells without quality material. That would be like having the blueprints to a nice home but having poor quality material to build it. It just couldn't be done. Therefore, diet is important.

Learn about nutrition, and eat properly. Your cells are about 75% to 85% water. Therefore, drink plenty of good, clean, pure water—about two quarts a day. Don't make your body have to get its water from colas, coffee and tea.

Exercise is also important to good health. One should do enough physical exercise every day to get the blood pumping well. Not exercising is like loading the trucks with good material to go to the building site but never moving the trucks. When you eat properly and drink plenty of water, you are loading the trucks; but if you do not exercise, the trucks do not get to the building site.

When you exercise, breathe deeply through your nose and exhale through your mouth. Get plenty of fresh air. Take long walks outside, and breathe deeply as you walk.

If you don't take good care of your health, you'll bear the physical consequences. First Corinthians 3:16, 17 says, "Know ye not that ye are the temple of God, and that the Spirit of God dwelleth in you? If any man defile the temple of God, him shall God destroy; for the temple of God is holy, which temple ye are."

In essence, these verses are simply saying that, if one does not take care of his body, he'll be destroyed physically. It's a matter of cause and effect.

It's a sad fact that most people take better care of their automobiles and their animals than they do their own bodies.

Joining in singing with Dr. Roberson as
Dr. Al Smith leads

25

Be honest: always tell the truth.

Make honesty a part of your character. Fight never to yield to the temptation to be dishonest. Sometimes the truth hurts. But in the long run, it never hurts as badly as being dishonest.

If someone catches you in a falsehood, it almost destroys, if indeed it doesn't destroy, your credibility with that person. And he will find it difficult to trust you the next time.

The board of a certain company was meeting, trying to decide what to do. When one member suggested that honesty is the best policy, the chairman of the board quickly asked, "And what's the next best policy?"

Honesty is not only the best policy; it should be the only policy.

It pays to be honest, but we should not be honest because it pays: we should be honest because it is right. If you are honest simply because it pays, you are not honest but greedy.

Is this a proud grandfather or what?
(Jana Kay Camperson)

26

Be balanced.

One of the most difficult things to maintain is balance. It requires constant effort.

Did you ever try to balance a broom on the end of your finger? If you did, you know that it requires constant correction in every direction. First, you must move the finger forward, then backward, then to one side and then the other. You can't hold the finger still and balance the broom.

The same is true in life. If one is to maintain a balanced life, he must quickly and constantly make corrections. It is easy to go too far in one direction or the other—eating too much and not taking enough time for exercise, or playing too much to the neglect of reading and studying, and so on.

Life can sometimes be like the pendulum on a clock, swinging from one side to the other. If you're over-disciplined as a child, it is likely that you'll be too easy on your children, and they will not get enough discipline. And the opposite is true. For one who is not disciplined, the chances are he'll be too strict on his children.

Balance! That's the important thing. I think that's what the Bible means when it says in Philippians 4:5, "Let your moderation be known unto all men."

27

"I'm glad to see you all here."

Leave all your options open for as long as you can.

Never close the door on any option until you have to. This way the opportunity is always there, if you want to take advantage of it later.

When I was pastor of a church in Decatur, Georgia, we signed a contract to buy property on which to build a church. But when we went for the closing, the man who ran the title on the property found that someone had an option to purchase the property, and the option had not expired.

When they called the individual to make sure that he wasn't going to exercise his option before giving us a clear title to the property, they discovered that the man was indeed going to exercise his option. He had taken the option three years earlier when property was less expensive. In the meantime, the price of the property had almost doubled in value. So, in essence, the man doubled his money by keeping his option open.

We had to buy another piece of property for the church site—which, by the way, turned out to be a better location for us.

"Will this one pass the test, Alan?"
(Alan Camperson)

28

Laughter is a good medicine.

Proverbs 17:22 says, "A merry heart doeth good like a medicine: but a broken spirit drieth the bones." It has been proven that laughter causes the body to help mend itself.

A hospital did a study on patients they considered to be terminally ill, and those who were physically able were taken to a theater-like room in the hospital and shown old Amos and Andy movies, the Three Stooges, the Little Rascals and others that caused them to laugh. The patients were put through this kind of therapy every day, and it was discovered that, after the experiment, they were showing improvement.

Of course, we know the Bible is right; and if it says, "A merry heart doeth good like a medicine," we can rest assured that laughter not only is good for the soul, it is also good for the body.

Learn to laugh at good, clean fun. Learn to laugh at yourself. Learn to appreciate and enjoy a good, clean joke. And remember, some of the funniest things in life are things that really happened.

My wife and I were watching a sports event on television when the camera zoomed in on an alligator in a big lake. The gator's head was barely coming up out of the water, and you could see its eyes and a part of its snout, along with a small part of its back. Of course, the water was blue; and whatever it was appeared to be in the sky, not in a lake.

My wife said, "That's a funny-looking airplane!"

And I calmly replied, "That's not an airplane; it's an alligator." Immediately we both began laughing. At the moment it seemed to be very funny, and we laughed until we actually cried.

For a long time afterwards, if I wanted a good laugh or wanted to cause her to laugh, I'd simply say, "That's a funny-looking airplane!" and immediately we'd both begin laughing.

You've had similar experiences. Remember them. Remember little statements that trigger you to laugh; and when you need a good laugh, use them.

You may not believe this, but it was but a few minutes after the above experience when company came in—my brother and sister-in-law. After some conversation my brother told the story about a man named Art. It was something rather serious, but in the midst of the story my wife asked, "Well, what is his name?"

Again it occurred to me as very funny, and I began to laugh. When I did, my brother and sister-in-law both began to laugh; and we laughed for the longest time. When we finally stopped, I told them the story about the alligator, and we all laughed again.

During their entire visit of two days, one of us would occasionally say, "Well, what's his name?" or, "That's a funny-looking airplane!" and again we'd all begin to laugh.

Don't confuse seriousness with solemnity. A man can be solemn without being serious and serious without being solemn. Nobody was more solemn than Bill Clinton when he said during the presidential campaign, "I will not raise the taxes on the middle class." But we all learned that he wasn't serious.

Don't confuse solemnity with spirituality. You don't have to look like you just fell out of the back end of a hearse to be a good Christian. Evangelist Fred Brown said, "Some people have a face so long that you could throw it out the window and use it for a fire escape."

Claiming precious promises
(son, Tony)

Always do
your best.

29

133

Dr. Bob Jones, Sr., used to say, "To do less than your best is a sin." God expects every individual to live up to his full potential. *Your* best may not be *the* best; but if it's your best, it will be God-blessed.

In Mark 14:8 Jesus said of Mary of Bethany, "She hath done what she could." In other words, she had lived up to her full potential. To be sure, there were some who were financially able to do more than Mary did, but no one can do more than live up to his or her full potential.

A Bantam chicken is a much smaller chicken than a Rhode Island Red. However, just like the Rhode Island Red, the Bantam also lays an egg. But its egg is smaller.

I have asked congregations, "Why do you think God made a Bantam chicken? Do you think He made a mistake and realized that He didn't make it big enough, so He started over and made larger chickens such as the Rhode Island Red and White Leghorn?"

Of course not. God doesn't make mistakes. He knows the end from the beginning. He made Bantam chickens because He wanted some Bantam eggs, and He never expected the Bantam to lay a Rhode Island Red egg.

The point is, the Bantam does her best, and so does the Rhode Island Red; and that's all God expects of either.

I heard of a rooster that saw an ostrich egg for the first time. He couldn't believe his eyes. Rolling the egg back into the henhouse, he called the chickens together and said, "Now, sisters, I don't want you to think I'm complaining, but I want you to see what they're doing in other places."

He was trying to motivate those White Leghorns and Rhode Island Reds to lay ostrich eggs. But no matter how hard they tried, they were limited. If they tried and failed, they would need to be psycho-analyzed. And if they tried and succeeded, the Lord knows they would need major surgery.

Do your best, and God will reward you based not upon what you've done but upon what you've done in light of what you could have done.

This applies to the little things as well, whether it be mowing the lawn, washing the dishes, preparing your lessons, or whatever. Do your best.

The Scripture says in Colossians 3:23, "Whatsoever ye do, do it heartily, as to the Lord, and not unto men."

Enjoying a good story with Mrs. Hutson
and Mrs. John R. Rice

30

Be yourself.

Did you ever hear it said of someone, "When God made him, He threw the mold away"? Well, that is true of every individual who has ever lived or ever will live. When God made you, He threw the mold away. You're the only you there will ever be. Everyone is an original. God does not make copies.

The expression, "identical twins," is a misnomer. There is no such thing. Every individual has his or her own RNA and DNA that is totally distinct from any other person who has ever lived or ever will live. Now if God determined to make every one of us different, then why should any one of us try to be a copy of someone else?

The Lord gave us four children, and not one of them was like another. Some required more discipline than others. Some were more sensitive. Others were more musically inclined. I never tried to mold any of them to be like someone else, but I often said, "I'll do anything I can to help you reach your full potential and be everything God wants you to be."

I think parents make a mistake when they try to fulfill their own ambitions through the lives of their children or grandchildren. Let them prayerfully choose their own vocation or surrender to their own calling. Then do whatever you can to help them reach their full potential.

And whatever you do, be yourself. Learn from others, but don't try to mimic others. When you try to be someone else, then in reality you're no one at all. You're certainly not yourself, and you're not the person you're trying to be. So be yourself.

B. R. Lakin, a famous evangelist, used to say, "If I

could only play one note on the piano, it would be the note B-natural."

31

"If you think about it, you'll get
that one later."

Don't overkill.

One can kill a mouse with a broom or even a rolled-up newspaper. He can also kill a mouse with a 22 rifle or a shotgun. Then, too, he could kill a mouse with a hand grenade. But if he does, he'll not only get the mouse, he'll get the house!

Some men were arguing about how to kill a hog. Several suggestions were made. Then finally one man convinced them to tie two sticks of dynamite around the hog's head and ignite it. Another argued that more dynamite was needed, but finally they settled on the two sticks.

Attaching a long fuse, they got far enough away so as not to be damaged from the explosion. And a few seconds after the fuse was lit, the dynamite exploded, and the hog completely disappeared. They couldn't even find one of its ears.

The man who argued for four sticks of dynamite rather than two said, "I told you we should have used more dynamite! You see, he got away!"

Don't overkill when disciplining a child. Never discipline one iota beyond the point where you get results. After all, results are what you're seeking. If one tap on the back of the hand will cause the child to pull the hand back and leave the flower arrangement alone, then one tap is all that's needed. If it takes two taps, then wait a few moments to see if he's going to respond to the first tap before tapping him again.

As soon as you get results, stop.

The same is true when arguing a point. Never say more than you have to say to convince your opponent. Once he sees he's wrong, you need not argue the point any further. To do so only humiliates him and will probably make an enemy for life.

Ball teams have often been accused of running up the

score. That simply means, after they had the other team beaten, they left in their best players and continued to score and score until the game became lopsided. The opposing team always feels like they're being taken advantage of in such a case, and they remember such experiences.

The idea is to win, not to humiliate the other team.

If you have several good arguments for your case, present the weakest one first. If that doesn't work, then very deliberately and tactfully present your next best argument. If still no success, move on to the third best argument, always saving your best ammunition for last and hoping you'll never need it.

Don't present all your arguments at first, like the rapid fire of a machine gun. Give your first argument time to convince your opponent before moving to your second one.

The preacher trying to convince the congregation must not overprove his point. Sometimes he can use so many verses trying to prove one point that the congregation forgets what he's talking about. It's like the old adage, "They can't see the forest for the trees."

Prove your point and support it with Scripture. But don't overkill.

A preacher was invited to speak at a country church, so he made thorough preparations so as to convince the crowd. As a matter of fact, he overly prepared. However, because of adverse weather conditions, only one man showed up for the service. And because no one else was there, he suggested they cancel the service. To which the preacher replied, "No, I came to preach, and I'm going to preach." And with that he opened his Bible and preached for about an hour and a half, quoting every verse and using every illustration.

When he finally finished, the old farmer said, "Parson, when I take a wagonload of hay out to feed the cows and only one cow shows up, I don't give her the whole wagonload."

Remember, don't overkill.

Darlings Donna and Diana
(Janney)

32

Make it a habit to praise the Lord.

n Psalm 7:17 David said, "I will praise the Lord according to his righteousness: and will sing praise to the name of the Lord most high." The Psalms have much to say about praising the Lord. Read especially Psalm 150 where in six verses the word *praise* is found thirteen times. It closes with verse 6 by saying, "Let every thing that hath breath praise the Lord. Praise ye the Lord."

Now when I speak of praising the Lord, I do not mean only public expressions of praise. For instance, when you have prayed about a very important matter and God answers your prayers, praise Him for it. When you're reminded of His blessings in other areas, take time to praise Him.

I think I have praised the Lord more the last year than I ever have in my life, and I feel guilty that I did not praise Him more, earlier. Looking back, I now wish I had spent more time praising Him for the health that I enjoyed for fifty-eight years before being diagnosed with cancer.

Billy Bray, the Cornish miner, used to shout "Glory!" all the time. It was his way of praising the Lord. One day while he was visiting a dying lady in the hospital, she said, "Billy, if I had the strength, I'd praise the Lord." Billy replied, "It's a pity you didn't praise Him when you had the strength."

Some of the happiest moments of my life have occurred in the last year. It was those moments when I was alone with God and offering genuine praise, heartfelt praise, for the wonderful, wonderful things He has done for me. I think, when we get to Heaven, we'll wish we had praised Him more. I have an idea that, up in Heaven, they are praising the Lord.

147

Isaiah tells us in chapter 6 that the seraphim are flying around the throne of God, singing, "Holy, holy, holy!" What's wrong with saying, "Praise the Lord for good health! Thank the Lord for a good family! O Jesus, I praise You for the wonderful things You've done for me"?

I wish I had the vocabulary to express the praise that my heart feels. Sing the Doxology and sing it from your heart:

Praise God, from whom all blessings flow;
Praise Him, all creatures here below;
Praise Him above, ye heav'nly host;
Praise Father, Son, and Holy Ghost.

Don't be a dead, dull, drab, dry Christian who thinks that all praise is shallow emotionalism. Learn to say, "Praise the Lord!" "Hallelujah!" and "Amen!" and express it when you feel it.

Dr. and Mrs. Roberson;
Dr. and Mrs. Hutson

33

Don't clog your soul.

Years ago I read this adage, "Faith is the intake and love is the outlet of the soul." If that is the case, then we must keep both the intake and outlet open.

Jesus said in Matthew 10:8, "Freely ye have received, freely give." We receive by faith, and we give because we love. Giving is an expression of love. I've often said that one can give without loving, but one cannot love without giving. The Scripture says in John 3:16, "For God so loved the world, that he gave his only begotten Son...."

Remember that we're not owners, we're stewards. Whatever we have—whether it be money, houses, cars, lands or whatever—it was entrusted to us by God, and we're expected to be good stewards. That is, we have received freely, so we should freely give.

Keep both the intake and the outlet of your soul open. The Dead Sea is dead because it only receives. It has no outlet. It never gives. And the soul that only receives sooner or later, in a sense, becomes a dead soul.

As you get older, your capacity to earn income increases. And usually, with the children grown and married, your financial needs decrease. The result is, you have more to give.

When that is the case, you ought to give more. But be sure you make wise investments. God will hold you responsible for how you invest the money He has entrusted to you as His steward. Support only ministries and causes in which you have complete confidence and with which you wholeheartedly agree. Don't use your money to support a preacher who does not believe the Bible is the Word of God or a cause that runs contrary to the clear teachings of the Bible.

In my opinion, the wisest investment is in the souls of men. Support soul-winning ministries. Use your dollars to win souls to Christ. In doing so, you're making friends who will greet you on the other side when you leave this body and move out for Heaven.

In Luke 16:9 the Scripture says, "Make to yourselves friends of the mammon [money] of unrighteousness; that, when ye fail [die], they may receive you into everlasting habitations." I take the verse to mean that we are to use our money to win souls to Christ so that, when we fail or die, they will receive us into Heaven—the everlasting habitation.

Don't let your soul get clogged. Keep both the intake and outlet open.

I once said to my wife, "Let's be a-givin' while we're livin', and we'll be a-knowin' where it's goin'." As you learn to give and give more, you'll find that Acts 20:35 is really true: "It is more blessed to give than to receive."

You'll also learn that the more you give, the more you'll have. John Bunyan once said,

> There was a man in our town
> (Some folks did think him mad);
> The more he gave away,
> The more he had.

You cannot outgive God. He will be no man's debtor.

Sharing a happy occasion with Dr. John
Reynolds, long-time associate

34

Communicate a clear message.

You are not only responsible for what you say; you are also responsible for what people understand you to say, so make sure that the message is clear. This is true when communicating with a child or an adult. If you have to ask several times, make sure they understand what you're trying to communicate.

A man once said, "I know you think you understood what I said, but I'm not so sure that what you understand is what I meant."

Of course, the most important message to communicate is the Gospel. The gospel message and what one does about it determines whether he or she will spend eternity in Heaven or Hell. So someone's eternity hinges on the message being communicated clearly.

Ephesians 2:8, 9 says,

"For by grace are ye saved through faith; and that not of yourselves: it is the gift of God: Not of works, lest any man should boast."

Salvation is entirely of grace. Grace means unmerited favor. It means that salvation is a free gift, and all one can do is receive it. If he had to do anything in exchange for it, it would not be grace but rather works.

Romans 11:6 says, "And if by grace, then is it no more of works: otherwise grace is no more grace. But if it be of works, then is it no more grace: otherwise work is no more work."

There can be absolutely no mixture of works and grace. It has to be one or the other. It cannot be any combination of the two.

In my opinion, more people are lost because of a wrong message than for the lack of any message at all. In Matthew 7:22,23 Jesus said,

"Many will say to me in that day, Lord, Lord, have we not prophesied in thy name? and in thy name have cast out devils? and in thy name done many wonderful works? And then will I profess unto them, I never knew you: depart from me, ye that work iniquity."

Here were people who evidently were trusting in their good works for salvation; and Jesus said, "I never knew you: depart from me, ye that work iniquity." The message that we are to communicate to men is the message of salvation by grace through faith. Learn the message and present it clearly. Don't give men a false hope of Heaven by getting them to trust anything other than Jesus Christ Himself for salvation.

A man is better off with no hope than a false hope. If he has a false hope of Heaven, he will go through life thinking he is saved, only to hear Jesus say, "I never knew you: depart from me, ye that work iniquity." But if he has no hope at all, there is a better likelihood that he will listen to somebody with the true message and trust Jesus Christ as Saviour.

40 years and still in love

35

Don't worry.

The Creator tells us in Philippians 4:6, "Be careful for nothing. . . ." *Careful* means "to be filled with anxious care," and *nothing* means "not one thing." So you might understand the verse better if I said, "Don't worry about one single thing." But nearly everybody is worried about something all the time, and isn't it strange that the majority of things we worry about never really happen at all?

Many people have made themselves sick, and some have gone to an early grave, worrying about things that never occurred.

But wait a minute! We're not even to worry about real things, things that really happen. In the first place, worry won't keep it from happening, worry won't change it, and worry cannot fix it.

Jesus said in Matthew 6:27, "Which of you by taking thought can add one cubit unto his stature?" The expression, "taking thought," means "to be filled with anxious care." It means "to worry."

Jesus reminds us that we cannot add one cubit to our stature by worrying about it. No matter how much you worry, you're still the same height when it's all over. So worry really accomplishes nothing.

Someone said, "Worry is like a rocking chair: it gives you something to do but gets you nowhere."

Don't confuse worry with concern. It's right to be concerned over things that really matter. But concern is one thing, and worry is another.

In a sense, worry is the opposite of faith. In the same verse where God reminds us to be careful for nothing, He goes on to say, ". . . but in every thing by prayer and

159

supplication with thanksgiving let your requests be made known unto God." In other words, don't worry about it; pray about it. And when you pray, trust God to do what's best. If you go on worrying, it shows you're not really trusting the Lord.

A little girl broke the head off her doll, but she didn't worry about it. She went on playing as if nothing had happened. Her mother said, "You've broken the head off your doll. Aren't you upset?"

"No, ma'am," she said. "Daddy can fix it."

Immediately her mother said, "Oh, no, your daddy cannot fix that doll. You've not only broken its head from its body, but you've shattered it into 100 pieces. Your daddy can't fix it."

The confident little girl replied, "It had a head on it when Daddy gave it to me."

That night when her father came home, the mother told him the story, and his eyes filled with tears. The next day he drove many miles to the same place where he had purchased the first doll and bought another one exactly like it. He said, "I couldn't disappoint that girl. She believed in me."

Remember, no matter how bad may be the situation or how dim the outlook, Daddy can fix it. Our Father in Heaven can do "exceeding abundantly above all that we ask or think" (Eph. 3:20). The little girl wasn't worried over the broken dolly. She had faith in her father.

Faith and worry cannot stay in the same room together. When one comes in, the other must go.

> **The worry cow would have lasted till now**
> **If she hadn't lost her breath,**
> **But she thought that the hay wouldn't last all day,**
> **So she choked herself to death.**

36

A quiet moment in the hospitality room
before speaking at the Ladies' Jubilee

Learn from the mistakes of others.

A person can be wiser than his or her years if he or she will learn from the mistakes of others. Some lessons are hard learned, but they are long remembered. Every person has learned such lessons in life. And when he tells you about it, listen and learn lest you make the same mistakes.

It would be a wise habit to ask your relatives and trusted friends, "What's the most important lesson you ever learned from some of your mistakes in life?" And one would do well to listen to the answers and record them for his own personal benefit.

There will be time to discuss such things while you're driving with a friend, taking a walk with a relative, or having lunch with a respected businessman.

Don't feel that you must make all the mistakes yourself: learn from the mistakes of others.

"God said it; that settles it."

37

Make sure
you're not look-
ing through a
dirty window.

A lady once complained to a visitor about her neighbor's clothes that were hung on the line to dry. "Look," she said, "there are dirty spots all over those sheets and stains on the clothes. It looks to me like, if she were going to hang her laundry out, she would wash it clean before putting it on the line today." She complained for the longest time.

Finally her visitor walked over and raised the window; and, lo and behold, the sheets and clothes were spotless—not a single stain or dirty circle.

The visitor said, "It's not your neighbor's clothes but your windows that need cleaning."

Bob Jones, Sr., told the story of a man who complained about everything stinking. Finally he said, "The whole world stinks." Then someone discovered that the man had Limburger cheese in his mustache!

The person who is a cynic (critic) and finds something wrong with everything probably has a problem himself. It might be wise to check his own windows or perhaps his mustache. And once his windows are clean and his mustache free of Limburger cheese, things will look and smell a lot better.

Jesus said, "And why beholdest thou the mote that is in thy brother's eye, but considerest not the beam that is in thine own eye?" (Matt. 7:3). I suppose it's all right to help your brother get the mote out of his eye, but one must make sure that he doesn't have a beam in his own eye while trying to help his brother with the mote, lest he turn his head and knock his brother's brains out with the beam that is in his own eye.

167

Influencing future generations

Be complimentary.

38

I t would be good to set a goal to compliment at least three people a day. People like to hear nice things said about them. It lifts them up, encourages them and makes them appreciate you even more.

That's why politicians hold babies and compliment their beauty or pat a young man on the head and say, "Oh, this is a nice young man!"

I heard of a lady who always had something complimentary to say about everyone. One day the meanest man in town died. It seemed there was nothing at all good about him that anyone could say. And the town wondered what complimentary remark the lady could make about this particular individual.

When she was told of his death, she calmly replied, "He could whistle good."

One of his members said to a particular pastor, "You are a model preacher."

On the way home he asked his wife, "What was that Mrs. Brown said about me?" and his wife replied, "She said you were a model preacher." He enjoyed it so much he kept asking his wife, "What was that Mrs. Brown said about me?"

One day his wife tired of hearing the question, so she opened the dictionary to the word *model*; and when he came home and asked, "What was that Mrs. Brown said about me?" she replied, "Oh, she said you were a model preacher. By the way, the dictionary says, '*Model: a small imitation of the real thing.*'"

Another lady said to her pastor, "You are a warm preacher." He figured that out for himself. It means "not so hot."

Little children especially need compliments and encouragement, but so do young people and adults. So be complimentary.

"You have to keep in shape for
this grandpa thing!"
(Alan and Curt Camperson)

When you are complimented, a simple thank you is a suffi- cient response.

39

If someone compliments you about something, you need not go into a lengthy explanation by saying, "Well, it was nothing. I just happened to be there at that particular time, and I had the opportunity that no one else had and really had nothing else to do anyway, so I went ahead and did it." Sometimes when people are complimented, they even say, "Oh, I know you don't mean that! That's not true," and on and on and on.

However, a simple thank you is a sufficient response. Don't go into a lengthy discourse and try to appear overly modest or humble.

"I hate the Devil!"

40

Give people a way out.

Even a rat will fight back if you hem him up and give him no way out. Try to avoid issuing ultimatums if at all possible. Make your arguments when necessary, but don't feel that you must make your opponent crawl on his knees and admit that he or she was wrong.

Paul said in Galatians 6:1, "Brethren, if a man be overtaken in a fault, ye which are spiritual, restore such an one in the spirit of meekness; considering thyself, lest thou also be tempted."

Playing and singing with Sword workers

41

Have a firm handshake.

By a firm handshake, I don't mean that you should try to crush the other person's knuckles. I simply mean, don't give him your hand as if it were a dead fish.

A man must be careful when shaking a lady's hand. In most cases, she has on several rings; and if he squeezes too hard, he'll hurt her fingers. Otherwise, it should be firm.

A firm handshake indicates that it's real and genuine.

I have never verified the story, but somewhere I read that extending an empty hand meant peace. It began years ago when almost all people carried weapons for their personal protection. So extending an empty hand was, in essence, saying, "I mean no harm. I want peace."

Never without a song
(Alan Camperson and Dustin Janney)

42

Look people in the eye.

When someone is talking to you, or when you're talking to someone, always try to maintain eye contact. If the conversation is lengthy, of course, it's all right to glance away. But always look back at the person.

If you look away while someone is talking with you, it seems to indicate that you have no interest in what he or she is saying. And if you're trying to communicate with someone, it is difficult to get the message across if the person is looking away.

Many times, while preaching a sermon, I have knocked on the pulpit as if knocking on a door, simply to get the attention of the people. And I've often said, "Look up here a minute," and then continued with the message.

The same is true when witnessing to an individual. Many times I've said, "If you don't mind, look at me."

When our children were small, I never tried to communicate with them unless they were looking at me.

Looking people in the eye helps to communicate a clear message and demonstrates that we're interested in what others are saying to us.

Competitive fun
(Curt Camperson)

43

Live within your means.

Years ago I heard someone define *stress* as "not having enough resources to meet your needs." There was no stress in the Garden of Eden before the Fall of man. Everything Adam and Eve needed was at their disposal. No wonder they lived for hundreds of years and could have lived forever had they not sinned and been driven from the Garden!

If you go into the store to buy groceries and then learn at the checkout line that you've bought more than you have money to pay for, it causes stress. And when you buy so many things on time that you cannot make the payments at the end of the month, it causes stress.

I've known families to separate and homes to be torn apart simply because the couple would not live within their means. It's better to have a one-room house where you can stay warm and dry and have a place to sleep and eat and be able to pay your bills—with some left over—than it is to live in a ten-room house and not have enough money to pay your bills at the end of the month. As you get financially able, you can always move into a larger house.

When our oldest daughter married, I suggested to her and our new son-in-law that they purchase a used house trailer and live in it until it was paid for, at which time they could sell it and put the equity into a small home; and later, as that was paid for or they had enough equity invested, they could sell it and buy a larger place. They took my advice, bought the used trailer, lived in it for awhile, got it paid for, and then sold it for more than they gave for it and used the money as a down payment on a nice home.

People are a lot happier having less and living within their means than they are having more and living under constant stress with bills that they find it almost impossible to pay on time. Living within your means may require discipline, but you'll be the happier for it.

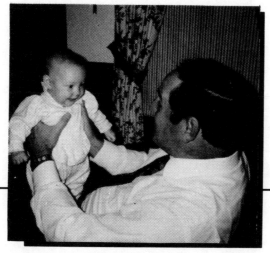

"PaPa's got the touch!"
(Jana Kay Camperson)

44

When someone
hugs you, let him
or her be first
to let go.

I have reference now to close friends and relatives. I have never been what you might call a "hugger"; but as I've gotten older, and especially during my serious illness, hugs have become very important to me; and I find myself hugging people whom I've never hugged before.

Hugging a child reassures him of your love. The same is true of a relative, close friend and especially one's own mate.

I have at least two grandchildren who, when they see Papa, will hug me for a long time; and, of course, I continue hugging as long as they do. I love it. I always let them be the first to let go.

If someone who loves you hugs you and you let go first, it seems to say, "That's enough," and it's almost like you didn't want him or her to hug you in the first place. Of course, there are exceptions to this rule; and it's especially true when you feel uncomfortable or have an uneasy feeling while someone is hugging you.

"Was that flash just for us, PaPa?"
(Tyler Chandler)

45

Smile a lot.

Some people find it easy to smile, but others, like myself, may have to work at it a little harder. My dear wife has a beautiful smile and smiles a lot at people. Dear Mrs. John R. Rice was the same way. I don't think I've ever seen a bad picture of Mrs. Rice, and the smile on her face was never a facade: it was genuine and real.

I have read that it takes more muscles to frown than it does to smile. I'm not sure that's true. But the person who frowns seems to get wrinkles in his or her face before the person who smiles a lot.

We used to have a little song we sang in the church. It went something like this:

> **You can smile, when you can't say a word;**
> **You can smile, when you cannot be heard;**
> **You can smile, when it's cloudy or fair;**
> **You can smile anytime, anywhere.**

We would then have the people sing the chorus and, rather than say the word *smile,* actually smile. It always turned out to be a fun part of the service, because many actually burst into laughter as they saw others trying to smile.

Like yawning, smiling is contagious. I have a friend in Atlanta whose last words are always "Keep smiling."

At the tomb of John Bunyan

46

Treat everyone
the way you
want to be
treated.

There are many wonderful principles in the Bible. If applied to one's life, they would cause him or her to be a much happier person. One such principle is sometimes called the Golden Rule. It is found in Matthew 7:12: "Therefore all things whatsoever ye would that men should do to you, do ye even so to them: for this is the law and the prophets."

Wouldn't it be wonderful if everybody in the world obeyed that little Bible principle! Just think! There would be no stealing, killing, vandalism, adultery nor many, many other things.

It is sad that we have come to a time in human history where a large segment of our society has no respect for human life or for people's property or anything else. Never do anything to anyone else you would not want him to do to you, and never treat him in a way that you would not want someone to treat you.

Holy Land travelers on the
Sea of Galilee

47

Never give up
on anybody:
miracles happen
every day.

This is especially true when dealing with Christians. Sometimes they get away from God. It looks as if they'll never come back. But Colossians 1:27 says, "...Christ in you, the hope of glory."

If a person has trusted Jesus as his Saviour, he or she may eventually stray far from God. But remember that Jesus in the person of the Holy Spirit came into that person the day he was saved, and He promised never to leave him.

Remember, too, that as long as He is there, there is still hope of glory in that person's life.

I'm thinking now of a man in the church where I was once the pastor. It seemed that this individual just kept making mistake after mistake and would never do right. Many times I've thought of "writing him off," so to speak, and never going back to visit him again. But today he is happy and is serving the Lord. The last time I saw him, he was in church with an open Bible in his hand and saying, "Amen," while the preacher delivered the sermon.

I recall taking a young man into our Christian school who had been kicked out of another Christian school in the Atlanta area. I talked with him and his parents and promised to do all I could to help him if he would cooperate.

That young man is now pastoring a church in a distant state and is running over 1200 in Sunday school.

I have read that Thomas Edison was sent home one day with a note pinned to his back: "Keep this boy at home; he's too dumb to learn." But today we enjoy over 1100 inventions that came from the brilliant mind of Mr. Edison.

Surrounded by love
(daughter Donna Janney, with Dustin, Denille, Derek and Diana)

Control your temper.

48

Some people seem to have shorter fuses than others, and they flare up and say things that they wish later had never been spoken. If two of this kind of people are together very long, they may wind up in a fistfight over something that wasn't even worth fussing about, let alone fighting about.

The Bible says in Colossians 3:13, "Forbearing one another, and forgiving one another, if any man have a quarrel against any: even as Christ forgave you, so also do ye." The word *forbearing* means to be extraordinarily patient. The person who does not control his temper cannot obey this verse.

A Christian once said to his friend, "I have a bad temper. I got it from my father."

His friend asked, "Have you been born again?"

"Oh, yes," he replied.

"Then," said his friend, "you didn't get it from your Heavenly Father."

"Mmm...that tastes good."

49

Vote.

I t is a sad fact that the majority of people in America never vote in any election, and political offices are held by people who get only a small percentage of the vote of those eligible to vote.

We sometimes think our vote does not count, but it's our way of expressing our opinion regarding elected officials.

In the 1994 Congressional Election, one congressional seat in the state of Connecticut was won by only four votes. At first it was only two votes; but after a recount, it turned out to be four.

It's our civic duty to exercise our right to vote. The person who does not vote has no right to complain about who holds elected offices.

Parents should encourage their children, as soon as they are old enough, to register to vote and then set the example by always voting. If your children are old enough to vote and are still at home, it's a wonderful thing for the entire family to go together to vote.

50

"O PaPa, <u>please</u> let me win once!"
(Curt Camperson)

Stop blaming others, and take responsibility for every area of your life.

It seems that many in our present society have been taught that everyone else is responsible for their wrongdoing. Some liberal explains that young girls have babies out of wedlock because they're poor. Others argue that violence on the streets is because people were raised in the wrong environment.

It's time for every individual to stop blaming someone else for his behavior and start taking responsibility for every area of his life. People do what they do because they choose to do it, not because they're poor or had to live in a certain neighborhood or environment.

When I was growing up, we lived in a two-room house—Mother, Daddy and all five children. We were poor, but we never used that as an excuse to steal, vandalize or commit some other crime. We were taught by our parents not to take things that belonged to others, not to use vulgar language or tell dirty jokes, etc. And we didn't do it, because we knew that, if our parents found out about it, we'd be strictly disciplined.

I can't imagine trying to explain to my father that I stole candy at the local grocery store because we were poor. To use an old Georgia expression, he would have "worn me out," then made me go to the local grocery store and apologize to the man who owned the store and ask what I could do to repay him, such as sweep the floor or some other chore. This wouldn't happen more than about once in a young child's life, and he'd learn not to take things that don't belong to him.

Forever Daddy's girl
(daughter Sherry Camperson)

51

Use your wit to amuse–not abuse.

It's all right to joke about someone you love, and whom everyone else knows you love, as long as it's kept in line. Both the person and those listening will laugh. But it's wrong to try to get a laugh at someone else's expense.

My wife is a funny person, and I often tell things she does that we both laugh about; and it causes others to laugh also. But if she ever indicated that she was not enjoying it, I would stop immediately.

One man, trying to be funny, put his fork into a piece of meat, held it up over his plate and said to his wife, "Is this pig on this fork?"—to which she quickly asked, "To which end of the fork are you referring?" He got what he deserved.

Enjoying Dr. Tom Malone's preaching

52

Make children aware of your knowledge of their wrongdoing.

Sometimes children will do things that don't deserve discipline, and a parent is inclined just to ignore it. But the child should always be made aware of the fact that the parent knows about his or her wrongdoing. If not, the child may think he's gotten away with something and the next time could be tempted to do something worse.

Simply get the child alone and say, "Now I want you to understand something: I know that you took an extra cola and drank it when I told you, you could have only one. I'm not going to spank you for it, but I want you to know that I do know it. And the next time you won't get off this easy."

The same holds true with people who work for you. Someone in your employment may do something that wasn't exactly right, but it wasn't bad enough to discipline him about it. However, in a nice, kind way, he should be made aware of your knowledge of the fact.

More than once in my life I've said to individuals, "Now I instructed you to do such-and-such a thing several weeks ago. And when the work came back through, it wasn't exactly like I told you to do it. It's no major thing, but the next time, be sure you do it exactly like I asked you to." This way the employee is aware that nothing is getting by you, and it will help him or her to be a better employee.

Subscriptions, subscriptions, subscriptions!

53

Salt is not antiseptic; it is aseptic.

n Matthew 5:13 Jesus said, "Ye are the salt of the earth." Salt is not antiseptic but aseptic. It doesn't cure corruption; at best it only prevents the spread of it.

I've talked with preachers involved in movements that tolerated liberals and modernists and had them argue that they were going to change the movement. I remember very well saying to one such preacher, "I hope you can change it, and I hope you'll prove me wrong; but you must remember that we're the salt of the earth, and salt doesn't cure corruption. At best it only prevents the spread of it."

I said, "You'll never change an apostate, modernistic organization."

In Matthew 9:16, 17 the Bible says,

"No man putteth a piece of new cloth unto an old garment, for that which is put in to fill it up taketh from the garment, and the rent is made worse.

"Neither do men put new wine into old bottles: else the bottles break, and the wine runneth out, and the bottles perish: but they put new wine into new bottles, and both are preserved."

Once an organization has been infiltrated with liberals who do not believe the Bible is the Word of God, it is impossible to change it. Harvard, Yale, Oberlin, Vanderbilt University and many other great schools were started by good, Bible-believing, fundamental people; but through the years, liberals infiltrated and took over, and in most cases these schools today have no idea why they were even started.

You can never turn any of them back into spiritual centers, training preachers and Christian workers. We must get the new bottle and a new garment. The old cannot be patched up.

Blessings—godly work and godly family

54

"Follow your conscience" is not always good advice.

233

You've heard people say, when asked about a certain thing, "Just follow your conscience." But one must remember that the conscience is not legislative; it is judicial. It does not make the laws; it only makes decisions based on its knowledge of the law. Therefore, if the conscience is not properly educated, then the man could follow his conscience in the wrong direction.

For instance, I've never been to a Catholic Mass, and my conscience does not bother me because I have been taught differently. On the other hand, if a good Catholic failed to attend Mass, his conscience might bother him, because he has been taught that one ought to go to Mass.

The only thing one can follow without getting into trouble is the Bible. A well-educated conscience is a very important thing to an individual. That is why parents must begin early to teach their children right from wrong. And this teaching must always be based on what the Bible says.

I could never get drunk because my conscience would bother me. Why? I was taught that drinking is wrong. I could never harm anyone physically. Why? Because my conscience would bother me. I was taught that we are not to inflict physical harm on people. On the other hand, today people do what they call "drive-by shootings," taking the lives of innocent people; and they never think anything about it. The problem is, they have never been taught morals based on the Bible. Therefore, their conscience doesn't bother them; it doesn't hurt them to see somebody else suffer.

So never say, "Follow your conscience"; always say, "Follow the Bible." And keep your conscience well educated by reading the Bible so that you make the best decisions based on the knowledge of the law.

The judge makes the decision after hearing the case. Sometimes the case is appealed, and a higher court reverses the lower court's decision because it had a better knowledge of the law than the lower court.

It is impossible to overstress the importance of a well-educated conscience.

"All right, let's go to work!"

Enjoy a good meal with a friend or friends as often as you can.

Whenever possible, enjoy a special meal with a good friend or friends. Make the place you eat a happy, bright and decorative place, a spot where you enjoy sitting. Don't rush your meal. Make it a time of fellowship and special occasion with that particular friend or friends. Perhaps a late breakfast would be a good time to have such a meal. I've noticed in most restaurants, where I've tarried and eaten, that the breakfast table seems to have a brighter setting of dishes. Even the tablecloths are brighter. Make these occasions very special times with your friends.

If there are things you wish to discuss, jot them down before the meal begins. But don't mention them during the meal. Once the meal is over and you're having a second cup of coffee or tea, then feel free to discuss the things you want to discuss.

People are so busy today that we don't have time to fellowship with one another. We grab a sandwich at a fast-food place, not only for breakfast but usually two or three meals a day. Mealtime should be a leisure time, a happy time.

Even when you are eating in restaurants, you are often rushed after having to wait in line. And there are so many noises and distractions that one can hardly fellowship. Having special people into your home will make them feel special.

Since my illness, when I have been somewhat confined, I've especially enjoyed having breakfast with my grown daughters who take turns spending some time with me. And occasionally I'll invite a friend over to join us for breakfast.

I didn't realize how much conversation I had missed out on with special people. Starting out as a teenage husband, father and preacher, wanting to "make my mark in life," so to speak (in other words, I wanted to be successful as God's servant), I didn't take enough time for these special occasions.

I cannot imagine the marriage supper of the Lamb being some kind of a hectic event when we are racing to see who can finish first, but a time when every moment is enjoyed by everyone who's present. I want to make every mealtime a happy time but especially these special occasions when we have visitors in.